TOP 10
SPORTS
★STARS★

BASEBALL'S
TOP
10
HOME RUN
HITTERS

Ken Rappoport

Enslow Publishers, Inc.
40 Industrial Road
Box 398
Berkeley Heights, NJ 07922
USA

http://www.enslow.com

Library of Congress Cataloging-in-Publication Data

Rappoport, Ken.
  Baseball's top 10 home run hitters / Ken Rappoport.
      p. cm. — (Top 10 sports stars)
  Includes bibliographical references and index.
  Summary: "A collective biography of the top 10 home run hitters, both past and present,
which includes accounts of game action, career statistics, and more"—Provided by
publisher.
  ISBN 978-0-7660-3465-5
  1. Baseball players—United States—Biography—Juvenile literature. 2. Baseball players—
Rating of—United States—Juvenile literature. 3. Home runs (Baseball)—Juvenile
literature. I. Title. II. Title: Baseball's top ten home run hitters.
  GV865.A1R345 2011
  796.3570922—dc22
  [B]
                                    2009027176

Printed in the United States of America

022010 Lake Book Manufacturing, Inc., Melrose Park, IL

10 9 8 7 6 5 4 3 2 1

To Our Readers:

We have done our best to make sure all Internet addresses in this book were active and
appropriate when we went to press. However, the author and the publisher have no
control over and assume no liability for the material available on those Internet sites or on
other Web sites they may link to. Any comments or suggestions can be sent by e-mail to
comments@enslow.com or to the address on the back cover.

♻ Enslow Publishers, Inc., is committed to printing our books on recycled paper. The
paper in every book contains 10% to 30% post-consumer waste (PCW). The cover board
on the outside of each book contains 100% PCW. Our goal is to do our part to help young
people and the environment too!

Illustration Credits: Associated Press / World Wide Photos.

Cover Illustration: Associated Press / World Wide Photos.

TOP 10

CONTENTS

Since Babe Ruth started drawing big crowds with his big bat in the 1920s, the home run has meant more to baseball than just about any other individual achievement. What can be more exciting than the crack of the bat and the ball flying to the far reaches of a baseball stadium?

Ruth came along at a time when baseball really needed him. Fans had lost faith in the game following the "Black Sox Scandal." In 1919, eight players from the Chicago White Sox had made a deal with gamblers to purposely lose the World Series to the Cincinnati Reds.

With the New York Yankees, Ruth's explosive bat and colorful personality helped to revive the sport following the scandal. Ruth's home run battles with Yankees teammate Lou Gehrig were memorable, adding more glory and goodwill to the sport. Fans came back to the ballparks, beginning to forget the cheating scandals of the past.

Many years after Ruth helped to save the game, baseball was again in need of goodwill in the 1990s following labor problems that canceled the World Series. This time, Mark McGwire and Sammy Sosa engaged in a stirring battle for the home run crown in 1998. Unfortunately, this took place during the "Steroid Era." There were investigations into the use of drugs by players—drugs that built up their bodies and strength and helped them hit more home runs.

The federal government has linked Barry Bonds to illegal, performance-enhancing substances beginning sometime around the 1999 season, while Alex Rodriguez has admitted to using the steroid "boli" between 2001 and 2003. The full extent of the use of performance-enhancing substances by other record-setting players during this era remains uncertain.

Through the years, things have changed in baseball. But the home run remains the most exciting element of the game. Now, from the Babe to Bonds, meet some of the game's all-time greatest sluggers.

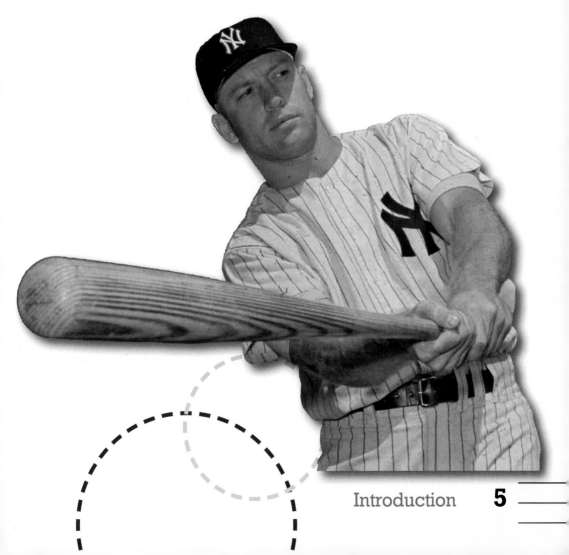

HANK AARON

HANK
AARON

Hank Aaron had ended the 1973 season two homers shy of breaking baseball's most hallowed record. It was not a pleasant off-season for Aaron.

He received death threats and hate mail from racists who did not want to see an African-American player surpass Babe Ruth's home run record.

Following an off-season that seemed to last forever and then spring training, the Atlanta Braves' star wasted little time in tying Ruth's record of 714 with a homer against the Cincinnati Reds in his first at-bat of the 1974 season.

Aaron failed to homer in another game

against Cincinnati, then sat out the third game of the series before returning home. He hoped to hit the record-breaker in front of the loyal Braves fans in Atlanta.

The road to the top was not easy for Aaron, a native of Alabama who played both baseball and football as a youth. He faced racial discrimination while playing for a Boston Braves farm team in the South during the 1950s. That made him all the more determined to succeed in the sport he loved best.

By the 1953 season, the Braves had moved from Boston to Milwaukee. Meanwhile, Aaron was moving up swiftly in the Braves' system. In 1954, Aaron was promoted to the major leagues.

Aaron's consistency was amazing: He is the only player in major league history with at least 30 home runs in each of his first fifteen seasons. In 1974, the player known as "The Hammer" was now forty and nearing the end of his career with the major league home run record within his sights.

Aaron faced pitcher Al Downing of the Los Angeles Dodgers on April 8, 1974. It was the fourth inning. Downing threw his first pitch to Aaron in the dirt. Ball one. Then Downing wound up and fired a fastball—down the middle of the upper part of the strike zone. The crack of the bat told the story: the ball sailed 400 feet, carrying over the left-center field fence in a misty rain at Atlanta Stadium for Aaron's 715th homer!

The record-breaker touched off one of the biggest celebrations sports fans had ever seen in Atlanta. Aaron was celebrating, too—inside. As he made an unemotional trip around the bases, as was his style, he remembered, "I just wanted to make sure I touched them." Then everyone wanted to touch Aaron, who was escorted to home plate by a couple of teenagers who had broken from the stands.[1]

Aaron would hit 40 more homers, finishing his career with 755 after moving on to the Milwaukee Brewers. None would compare with No. 715, though. "Now I can consider myself one of the best," said Aaron in a rare moment of self-praise.[2]

HANK AARON

BORN: February 5, 1934, Mobile, Alabama.

PRO CAREER: Milwaukee Braves, 1954–1965; Atlanta Braves, 1966–1974; Milwaukee Brewers, 1975–1976.

RECORDS: Ranks No. 2 on the all-time home run list with 755. Among numerous other achievements, Aaron is the all-time leader in runs batted in with 2,297 in his twenty-three-year career.

BARRY BONDS

BARRY
BONDS

"Batting for San Francisco . . . Barry Bonds!" A cheer went up at AT&T Park in San Francisco as the Giants' slugger stepped to the plate.

It was the night of August 7, 2007 and Bonds needed just one more home run to break Hank Aaron's career record of 755. The chase for baseball's most cherished record had made Bonds the center of attention everywhere.

And now, at the age of forty-three, he was nearing his goal. Just one more home run would do it, as he had done 755 other times in a long and controversial career. In came the pitch from the Washington

Nationals' Mike Bacsik. Out went the ball—a drive to the deepest part of AT&T Park, 435 feet into the right-center field seats.

Bonds' home run chase had been a distraction to his Giants teammates. Now the media could focus on the pennant race instead, and on baseball's investigation of a drug scandal that had rocked the sport. Bonds was one of several players called to testify before a congressional committee investigating steroid use in baseball.

Born in Riverside, California, Bonds came from a baseball family. His father, Bobby, was an All-Star outfielder with the Giants, among other teams. Between them, Barry and his father hit more than 1,000 home runs! That was more than any other father-son duo in baseball history.

Some players in Major League Baseball underwent dramatic physical changes in the 1990s, becoming bigger and stronger. Bonds was one of them. When he made his major league debut with the Pittsburgh Pirates in 1986 following a great college career at Arizona State, he weighed 185 pounds and hit only 16 home runs in 113 games.

Things began to change for Bonds after he left Pittsburgh to sign a then-record $43.75 million free-agent contract with the Giants in 1993. By 2001, Bonds had bulked up to a muscular 228 pounds and hit a major league record 73 homers in 153 games.

He had suddenly become the most feared slugger in the game. While most sluggers start to slow down at the age of thirty-seven, Bonds continued to post amazing numbers. Until injuries slowed him down in 2005, Bonds continued to hit pitches into the seats with remarkable regularity. Then on the night of August 7, 2007, he walked into baseball history by breaking Aaron's career home run record.

"It's been fantastic," Bonds said after crossing home plate with his 756th home run.[1]

BARRY BONDS

BORN: July 24, 1964, Riverside, California.

· ·

PRO CAREER: Pittsburgh Pirates, 1986–1992; San Francisco Giants, 1993–2007.

· ·

RECORDS: Major League Baseball's all-time home run leader with 762. Set the single-season home run record with 73 in 2001, and won a record seven Most Valuable Player awards.

· ·

LOU GEHRIG

LOU
GEHRIG

It was Lou Gehrig Appreciation Day at Yankee Stadium. Thousands of fans waited as the New York Yankees' popular slugger stepped up to the microphone to make his farewell speech.

"For the past two weeks you have been reading about the bad break I got," Gehrig said. "Yet today I consider myself the luckiest man on the face of the earth."[1]

The luckiest man? Gehrig was battling a crippling muscular disease that left him weak and led to the end of his record playing streak of 2,130 games and his career with the Yankees. Yet he assured the fans that although he was quitting baseball, he was not quitting his fight against his disease.

The date was July 4, 1939. Two years later, Gehrig would die, a victim of amyotrophic lateral sclerosis (ALS). Little was known of the disease then, but the public became more aware of ALS after the death of the high-profile Gehrig. It later became known as "Lou Gehrig's Disease."

Lou became known as the "Iron Horse" while playing in every Yankees game for fifteen years. One of many highlights: four consecutive home runs in a game in Philadelphia's Shibe Park in 1932.

Considering that his career was cut short by illness, Gehrig's statistics are amazing. Usually batting after Ruth in the No. 4 cleanup spot, Gehrig drove in 1,990 runs, third highest in major league history. He hit 493 home runs and posted a lifetime batting average of .340, unusually high for a power hitter.

Talk about the Big Bang! Between the two of them, Gehrig and Ruth drove in 4,201 runs and hit 1,207 homers. They were the one-two punch of the famed 1927 "Murderers' Row" lineup that some consider the best team in baseball history.

Gehrig was a major part of six world champions and seven pennant winners. However, he is personally best known for his legendary consecutive playing streak that stood for fifty-six years before Baltimore's Cal Ripken, Jr. broke it in 1995.

It wasn't until the 1939 season that Gehrig suffered a drop-off in performance. It was dramatic. He felt weak.

He even struggled just to make simple put-outs at first base. One day Gehrig walked over to Yankees manager Joe McCarthy and told him he was taking himself out of the lineup.

A deeply saddened McCarthy replaced Gehrig at first base with Babe Dahlgren. He gave Lou the honor of taking the lineup card up to home plate as thousands of fans in Detroit applauded him for several minutes.

Then Gehrig returned to the dugout and walked out of baseball forever.

Lou GEHRIG

BORN: June 19, 1903, New York, New York.

· ·

DIED: June 2, 1941, New York, New York.

· ·

PRO CAREER: 1923–1939, New York Yankees.

· ·

RECORDS: Among numerous records—including most grand slams (23), and three of the top six RBI seasons in baseball history—Gehrig is most famous for his consecutive-game streak of 2,130, ultimately surpassed by Baltimore's Cal Ripken, Jr., in 1995.

· ·

JOSH GIBSON

JOSH
GIBSON

This is a story about the greatest home run hitter you never heard of. His name is Josh Gibson.

There is a reason you might never have heard of him: He played his entire career in the Negro Leagues. While most every baseball fan in America was following the exploits of the great white stars, African-American players remained on the outer edges of the national game. Gibson dreamed of playing in the major leagues, but died prematurely at the age of thirty-six—just a few months before Jackie Robinson broke the color line in baseball in the 1947 season.

A solid 6-foot-1, 215-pound catcher, Gibson was credited with all kinds of astonishing home run feats that—if true—would place him at the top of the all-time list. Yes, ahead of even Babe Ruth, Hank Aaron, and Barry Bonds. But records were loosely kept in the Negro League and Gibson's home run totals are debatable.

Was it 823 home runs, as some historians claim—84 of them in one season alone? More than 900, or closer to 1,000, according to others? Some conservative figures place his Negro League totals at much lower numbers, although his home run ratio ranks with the best in baseball. His plaque in the Hall of Fame may be closer to the truth—citing "almost 800" homers in his seventeen-year career.

There are countless stories of Gibson's monster home runs. Once, according to pitcher Satchel Paige, Gibson bounced the ball off the scoreboard clock in Chicago's Wrigley Field, 100 feet off the ground in straightaway center field. If the ball had been allowed to complete its route, it was estimated it would have traveled 700 feet! That would have eclipsed even Ruth's longest homers. With his powerful swing, Gibson made tape-measure homers of 500 feet or more almost an everyday occurrence.

"The stories about him hitting 500-foot home runs are all true," Roy Campanella, the late Brooklyn Dodgers catcher, once said. "I saw them."[1]

Gibson was more than just a home run hitter. In 1943, he posted a remarkable .517 batting average for the entire season. Although he played with several teams, Gibson was mostly known for his association with the Homestead Grays and Pittsburgh Crawfords of the Negro National League.

In 1972, twenty-five years after Gibson's death, the Hall of Fame opened its doors to the greatest home run hitter in Negro League history and perhaps in all of baseball.

JOSH GIBSON

BORN: December 21, 1911, Buena Vista, Georgia.

· ·

DIED: January 20, 1947, Pittsburgh, Pennsylvania.

· ·

PRO CAREER: Pittsburgh Crawfords, 1927–1929, 1932–1936; Homestead Grays, 1930–1931, 1937–1946.

· ·

RECORDS: The greatest home run hitter in Negro League history. Although records were loosely kept, Gibson's plaque in the Baseball Hall of Fame says he hit "almost 800 home runs" in his seventeen-year career.

· ·

KEN GRIFFEY, JR.

KEN
GRIFFEY, JR.

Only five other players had hit 600 home runs. Ken Griffey, Jr., needed only one more round-tripper to join that exclusive baseball club.

But after hitting No. 599 he was struggling— 26 plate appearances without a homer. Now Griffey's Cincinnati Reds were playing the Florida Marlins in Miami in the middle of the 2008 season, and Griffey was hoping to finally break his long-ball slump. Facing Marlins starter Mark Hendrickson, Griffey worked the count to 3–1. The next pitch was a curveball. Crack! The ball sailed off Griffey's bat over the fence in right field. Number 600 was in the books.

"I didn't really think about it running around the bases," Griffey said of his 600th homer. "I don't think I touched any of the bases. I sort of floated around."[1]

He was called the "Natural", the "Kid" and "Junior." As Ken Griffey's son, Ken Griffey, Jr., had big shoes to fill. Ken Griffey, Sr., had been a star outfielder with the Cincinnati Reds.

Selected as the number one pick in the amateur draft by the Seattle Mariners in 1987, Griffey didn't take long to establish himself as the premier player in baseball. He was a consistent .300 hitter in the 1990s, smashing 422 home runs in the decade.

One of his most memorable home runs did not count toward his career total. During the Home Run Derby at the 1993 All-Star Game in Baltimore, Griffey blasted a shot over the right field wall that hit a warehouse across the street from Camden Yards. It was one of the longest home runs ever seen in the Orioles' park.

With one of the smoothest swings in the game, Griffey was always regarded as classic in form at the plate. He reached 400 home runs faster than anyone. The next 100 were the toughest for Griffey. Once tabbed as the player most likely to break Hank Aaron's home run mark of 755, Griffey suffered a series of injuries that slowed down his chase for the record that Barry Bonds eventually broke.

It wasn't until late June of the 2004 season, on Father's Day, that Griffey finally reached the 500 mark. It had taken him more than four years to do it. Griffey had stayed free of serious injuries that season and regained his home run swing.

In the audience were Griffey's children and his father.

"It was a nice Father's Day present," said the elder Griffey.[2]

Griffey played through pain before finally reaching the 600 mark four years later. A remarkable achievement, considering his many injuries. That season, he was asked about his legacy. What would it be?

"That throughout everything he's gone through, he never gave up," Griffey told a reporter.[3]

KEN GRIFFEY, JR.

BORN: November 21, 1969, Donora, Pennsylvania.

PRO CAREER: Seattle Mariners, 1989–1999, 2009–2010; Cincinnati Reds, 2000–2008; Chicago White Sox, 2008.

RECORDS: American League Most Valuable Player in 1997, seven-time Silver Slugger Award winner as the top offensive player at his position. One of only six players in major league history to hit 600 home runs.

MICKEY MANTLE

MICKEY
MANTLE

They called Mickey Mantle
the "next Joe DiMaggio."
It was unfair.

As a nineteen-year-old rookie, he was already being compared to one of the greatest and most popular players in baseball history. But comparisons were expected. Mantle was ticketed to be the Yankees' center fielder of the future, replacing DiMaggio.

Like DiMaggio, Mantle was speedy and graceful, able to chase down long fly balls with seeming ease. And like DiMaggio, he had power at the plate, except that Mantle was a switch-hitter. He could bat from either side—right-handed or left-handed.

Mantle was from Oklahoma. A Yankees scout, impressed with Mantle's speed and his switch-hitting prowess, signed him to a contract following his graduation from Commerce High School. By the time he had worked his way up through the minors playing shortstop, Mantle was a star in waiting. DiMaggio called him "the greatest prospect I can remember."[1]

Although he could strike out as often as hit a towering home run, causing fans to boo him unmercifully, Mantle's awesome power eventually won those same fans over. Who could forget his famous clout off Kansas City A's pitcher Bill Fischer the night of May 22, 1963? The ball soared up and up, finally crashing against the upper façade of the right-field stands at Yankee Stadium, 108 feet above the playing field.

"It was the hardest ball I ever hit," Mantle said of the drive that was one of the longest in baseball history.[2]

When Mantle connected with his 33-ounce, 35-inch Louisville Slugger, the ball was usually long gone. While playing for the Yankees from 1951 to 1968, the center-field great put together a list of monster home runs that few can match. Mantle was at his best in the postseason, where he cracked a record 18 home runs in World Series play, helping the Yankees win seven titles.

In 1956, he accomplished that rarest of baseball feats, the Triple Crown, leading the American League in batting average, home runs, and RBIs. He accomplished many of his gigantic feats while playing in terrible pain from a number of injuries throughout his major league career.

Mickey Mantle earned a place as a star of stars in Yankee Stadium's Monument Park honoring the all-time Yankee greats. It was placed right alongside Babe Ruth, Lou Gehrig, and, of course, Joe DiMaggio.

MICKEY MANTLE

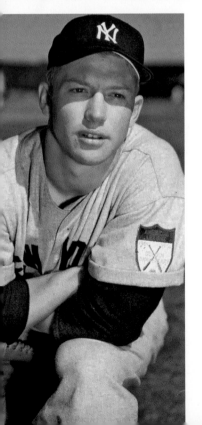

BORN: October 20, 1931, Spavinaw, Oklahoma.

. . . .

DIED: August 13, 1995, Dallas, Texas.

. . . .

PRO CAREER: New York Yankees, 1951–1968.

. . . .

RECORDS: Three-time American League MVP (1956, 1957, 1962), AL Triple Crown winner (1956), sixteen-time All-Star. Holds numerous World Series records, including most home runs (18).

. . . .

WILLIE MAYS

WILLIE
MAYS

On a steamy summer day in New York City's Harlem section, the shouts and laughter of kids playing stickball filled the air.

In the middle of them was one adult who seemed to be having more fun than anyone—Willie Mays, the New York Giants' great center fielder.

Mays might have been a little tired after a long day at the ballpark. But he still had plenty of energy left to participate in New York's popular street game with his neighborhood friends. Using a broom handle for a bat, Mays whacked a rubber ball far down the street.[1] It was the same way he hit a baseball to the far reaches of the Polo Grounds.

The enthusiastic Mays, known as the "Say Hey Kid" for his lively personality, was a pleasure to watch. One of the most exciting players the game has ever seen, Mays was a complete "five-tool player" who could hit for average, hit for power, field, throw, and run.

He smashed 660 homers among his 3,283 hits in the big leagues. He ran the bases with flair. He made memorable catches in the outfield. He had one of the strongest throwing arms in baseball. One of his most famous plays was made against the Cleveland Indians in the first game of the 1954 World Series. The score was tied 2–2 in the top of the eighth when the Indians put runners on first and second.

Vic Wertz smashed a long drive to center. It looked like it would clear the bases and give the Indians a 4–2 lead.

Mays had other ideas. With the crack of the bat, Willie turned and raced toward the deepest part of the Polo Grounds. The Polo Grounds was an oddly constructed baseball stadium that measured nearly 500 feet to the center field wall and much shorter distances down the foul lines.

Willie turned on the jets. Galloping toward straightaway center, he caught the ball over his left shoulder near the warning track. In one motion, he wheeled and fired the ball back toward the infield. Two runs were saved! The play highlighted the Giants' first-game victory. They went on to a four-game sweep of the heavily favored Indians.

At the plate, Mays also provided many dramatic moments while playing for the Giants in New York and after they moved to San Francisco in 1958. On the final day of the 1962 season, Mays hit his major league–leading 49th homer to salvage a tie for the pennant. The Giants went on to the World Series.

Mays won four home run titles and two MVP awards in his twenty-two-year big league career. And he enjoyed every minute.

WILLIE MAYS

BORN: May 6, 1931, Westfield, Alabama.

. . . .

PRO CAREER: New York/San Francisco
Giants, 1951–1952, 1954–1972; New York
Mets, 1972–1973.

. . . .

RECORDS: Two-time National League MVP
(1954, 1965), Gold Glove Award winner at
his center field position from 1957–1968,
and a record-tying twenty-four All-Star
appearances. Fourth in career home runs
with 660 and first player with 500 homers
and 3,000 hits.

. . . .

SADAHARU OH

SADAHARU

OH

The "King" held a Samurai sword
in his hand. He whipped the
instrument through a straw doll,
cutting it in half.

This was no scene from a Japanese action movie, but rather a scene in a baseball locker room. Sadaharu Oh, whose last name means king in Japanese, was practicing his swing. His *home run* swing. Cutting a straw doll in half with one swipe of the sword was one of many training techniques that would help Oh become the most feared slugger in Japanese baseball history.

By the time he retired in 1980 after twenty-two seasons with the legendary Yomiuri Giants of the Japan League, Oh had slammed 868 homers, more than the great Babe Ruth, Hank Aaron, or Barry Bonds—although it was hard to compare the quality of competition. And American ballparks were larger than Japanese ballparks then.

"Everything about the [major league] game is faster," Oh said in a 1998 interview with *Sports Illustrated*. "I was a fastball hitter, so it would have been quite a challenge. But I would have liked to have tried."[1]

Considering his poor start in Japanese professional ball, Oh hardly seemed destined for stardom. A left-handed hitter converted from a pitcher, Oh hit only seven home runs and compiled a woeful batting average of .161 in his first season, 1959. Three seasons later, he was on his way to his first of 13 straight home run titles.

What happened?

The "Flamingo" happened. That was what they called Oh's new batting stance suggested by a coach to cure a hitch in his swing. Oh held his right foot aloft, like the bird standing on one foot, as he patiently awaited the pitcher's offering. The stance was similar to one used by New York Giants Hall of Famer Mel Ott.

Oh, son of a Chinese father and Japanese mother whose birth name was Wang Chenchih, underwent other changes. Oh learned physical and mental exercises that helped him.

Oh dominated Japanese baseball for two decades with a fury unmatched in his sport's history. He won

15 home run titles, 13 RBI titles, 5 batting titles, 2 Triple Crowns and 9 Most Valuable Player awards. He was also one of the Central League's top defensive first basemen. He appeared in 18 All-Star games and led the Giants to 11 team championships with his bat and glove.

SADAHARU OH

BORN: May 10, 1940, Tokyo, Japan.

PRO CAREER: Yomiuri Giants, 1959–1980.

RECORDS: Averaged 45 homers a year, including a Japanese record of 55 in one season, to win thirteen straight home run titles. Won Triple Crowns in 1974 and 1975. With 868 home runs, Oh holds the all-time Japanese record.

ALEX RODRIGUEZ

ALEX
RODRIGUEZ

Wow! Fourteen home runs in
eighteen games. Alex Rodriguez
was off to one of the hottest starts
in major league history.

It was the 2007 baseball season and the New
York Yankees' slugger had tied the major
league record for most homers in April.

"I'm just trying to have fun," Rodriguez said of his great power show.[1]

Rodriguez was born in New York and lived
in the Dominican Republic before his family
settled in Miami. There, Rodriguez became a
local sports celebrity while starring for national
champion Westminster Christian High School.

He was regarded as the top baseball prospect in America. He was also a star football player. The University of Miami offered him a scholarship in both baseball and football. But the Seattle Mariners had picked him first overall in the 1993 amateur baseball draft. He decided to turn pro.

By 1996, Rodriguez had a breakthrough year: 36 homers, 123 RBIs, and a .358 batting average. It was the highest average for a right-handed hitter in the American League since Joe DiMaggio batted .381 in 1939.

Rodriguez had played shortstop throughout his major league career. But upon joining the Yankees in 2004, the Gold Glove shortstop became a third baseman. And his hitting continued to amaze baseball fans. In 2007, Rodriguez became the youngest player in the game's history to reach the 500-homer level. Rodriguez broke the record set by Jimmie Foxx in 1939.

In the off-season, the Yankees signed Rodriguez to a new, ten-year, $275 million deal just as they were building a new stadium. New contract, new stadium, and new possibilities. The future looked bright.

Suddenly, there was shocking news. In early 2009, Alex admitted to using steroids between 2001 and 2003 while playing for the Texas Rangers. People could only guess how much these performance-enhancing substances helped Rodriguez to hit his home runs.

Alex made a public apology and was prepared to contribute to charity and raise awareness about the steroid problem in baseball. It was rock bottom for A-Rod.

After recovering from hip surgery, Rodriguez returned in May and homered on the first pitch he saw. In the final game of the season, he hit two home runs in one inning to finish with 30 home runs and 100 RBIs—the twelfth season in a row he reached such numbers.

Then in the playoffs, he hit .365 with 6 home runs and 18 RBI in 15 games to help lead the Yanks to a World Series victory. The 2009 season proved to be a season of both fall and redemption for Alex Rodriguez.

ALEX RODRIGUEZ

BORN: July 27, 1975, New York, New York.

PRO CAREER: Seattle Mariners, 1994–2000; Texas Rangers, 2001–2003; New York Yankees, 2004–present.

RECORDS: Three-time American League MVP (2003, 2005, 2007). In 2007, as the Yankees' third baseman, Rodriguez tied the record for most homers in April with 14.

BABE RUTH

BABE RUTH

Babe Ruth heard the yells and name-calling from the Chicago Cubs' bench as he stepped into the batter's box at Wrigley Field.

It was the third game of the 1932 World Series and Ruth, the biggest star of the New York Yankees, had already taken two strikes. After the first strike, Ruth held up one finger. After the second, he held up two.

Ruth had also taken two balls for a 2–2 count. Before the next pitch, Ruth extended his arm. Was he pointing toward the center field bleachers?

The Cubs' pitcher wound up and fired.

Ruth swung and the crack of his bat could be heard all over the ballpark. The ball sailed higher and higher, landing in the deepest part of center field for a home run!

Did Ruth actually "call" the shot to center field? We may never know.

When Ruth retired in the midst of the 1935 season, the "Sultan of Swat" led the majors in home runs (714), runs batted in (2,211), runs scored (2,174) and walks (2,056). Ruth knew how to make an exit, hitting three home runs for the Boston Braves against the Pittsburgh Pirates on May 25, 1935.

It was with another Boston team that Ruth got his start when he signed with the Red Sox for the 1914 season as a pitcher. Although Ruth set World Series pitching records, it was his hitting that soon caught everyone's attention.

Imagine a player hitting more home runs in one season by himself than any other team in the major leagues. Ruth just about did that in 1920 when he hit 54, out-slugging every team in the majors but the Philadelphia Phillies, who had 64.

Babe came along just when baseball fans needed a hero. With his colorful, no-holds-barred personality and massive home runs, Ruth helped restore popularity to the game. Ruth's trade to the Yankees haunted the Red Sox for many years thereafter and became known as the "Curse of the Bambino." Ruth, in the center of the lineup with his big stick, led the Yankees to World Series triumphs in 1923, 1927, 1928, and 1932.

The 1927 Yankees featured a "Murderers' Row" lineup anchored by Ruth and Lou Gehrig, and is considered one of the greatest baseball teams of all time. That year, Ruth clouted 60 home runs, a record that stood for nearly four decades.

For many, the colorful "Bambino" still remains the greatest of them all for what he meant to the game.

BABE RUTH

BORN: February 6, 1895, Baltimore, Maryland.

DIED: August 16, 1948, New York, New York.

PRO CAREER: Boston Red Sox, 1914–1919; New York Yankees, 1920–1934; Boston Braves, 1935.

RECORDS: Ruth's record of 60 home runs in 1927 was the major league standard for thirty-four years. A star pitcher as well as a famous hitter with 714 career homers, Ruth is generally considered the greatest baseball player of all time.

CHAPTER NOTES

CHAPTER 1. HANK AARON

1. Wayne Minshew, "The Hammer Hits the Big One," *The Sporting News*, April 27, 1974.
2. Ibid.

CHAPTER 2. BARRY BONDS

1. The Associated Press, "Home Run King," August 9, 2007.

CHAPTER 3. LOU GEHRIG

1. Larry Schwartz, "Gehrig Legacy One of Irony," *ESPN.com*, n.d., <http://espn.go.com/sportscentury/features/00014204. html> (September 4, 2009).

CHAPTER 4. JOSH GIBSON

1. Rod Beaton, "If Bonds Passes Threesome, Legend of Josh Gibson Awaits," *USA Today*, August 15, 2002.

CHAPTER 5. KEN GRIFFEY, JR.

1. Mark Sheldon, "Griffey Joins Kings of Clout with No. 600," *MLB.com*, June 10, 2008, <http://www. mlb.com/news/article.jsp?ymd=20080609&content_ id=2879002&vkey=news_cin&fext=.jsp&c_id=cin> (September 4, 2009).
2. Chuck Johnson, "Junior's Achievement: 500 HRs," *USA Today*, June 21, 2004.
3. Hal Bodley, "Griffey Rises Above the Cloud," *USA Today*, June 29, 2007

CHAPTER 6. MICKEY MANTLE

1. "Legends: Mickey Mantle," *Zimbio*, November 18, 2008, <http://www.zimbio.com/Baseball/articles/124/ Legends+Mickey+Mantle> (September 2, 2009).
2. John Drebinger, "Mantle's Homer Subdues A's, 8–7", *New York Times*, May 23, 1963.

Chapter 7. WILLIE MAYS

1. Larry Schwartz, "Mays Brought Joy to Baseball," *ESPN.com.*, n.d., <http://espn.go.com/sportscentury/features/00016223.html> (September 4, 2009).

Chapter 8. SADAHARU OH

1. Richard Deitsch, "Sadaharu Oh, Home Run King," *Sports Illustrated*, October 5, 1998.

Chapter 9. ALEX RODRIGUEZ

1. Paul White, "How A-Rod Learned to Relax and Enjoy New York," *USA Today*, May 4, 2007, p. 1A.

Further Reading

Herzog, Brad. *The 20 Greatest Athletes of the 20th Century*. New York: Rosen, 2002.

Schwarz, Alan. *Baseball All-Stars: Today's Greatest Players*. New York: Sports Illustrated for Kids Books, 2002.

Will, Sandra. *Baseball for Fun!* Mankato, Minn.: Compass Point Books, 2003.

Internet Addresses

The Official Site of Major League Baseball
http://www.mlb.com/

The National Baseball Hall of Fame and Museum
http://www.baseballhall.org/